funky party

party food for happy children

To Mum, the source of my creativity... this one is for you. x

funky party

party food for happy children

mark northeast

absolute press  A.

First published in Great Britain in 2012
by Absolute Press, an imprint of
Bloomsbury Publishing Plc

Absolute Press
Scarborough House
29 James Street West
Bath BA1 2BT
Phone 44 (0) 1225 316013
Fax 44 (0) 1225 445836
E-mail info@absolutepress.co.uk
Website www.absolutepress.co.uk

Text copyright
© Mark Northeast, 2012
This edition copyright
© Absolute Press, 2012
Photography copyright
© Jason Ingram

Publisher Jon Croft
Commissioning Editor Meg Avent
Design Matt Inwood
Photography Jason Ingram
Food Styling Mark Northeast & Genevieve Taylor

ISBN 9781906650735
Printed in China by C&C Offset Printing Co. Ltd

let's party!

introduction

As a child growing up, we weren't spoilt when it came to birthdays. We were taught to appreciate the things we received and the birthday parties in our house were no different than that of other children growing up in the late seventies and early eighties. Of all the usual party food at the table – the crisps, the jelly and the sandwiches – one thing that could always be guaranteed was a great looking birthday cake.

Mum's hobby back then was decorating cakes and throughout my younger years I was probably told on more than one occasion to 'step away from the table' as Mum delicately placed petal after intricate petal on to the most exquisite looking wedding and birthday cakes. She would sit for hours icing decorative patterns and shaping different flowers and characters. To this day, she will still throw herself wholeheartedly into a craft project with the grandchildren, creating costumes, building models or just simply painting a picture.

I think that's where my creativity comes from, so too my attention to detail and now, in later life, my patience and determination to complete a project. (Those early years of Lego building tantrums are now but a distant memory.)

I remember making my first character cake with Mum for our primary school fête one summer. She helped make the chocolate sponge and then I carefully cut out a shape resembling E.T. the Extra-Terrestrial. I remember the pride of seeing it on display in the school hall with a '3rd Place' rosette next to it. My very first cake. I was 9 years old.

When it came to writing this book, I was both nervous and excited from the outset. The thrill of turning my ideas into food that would put smiles onto the faces of many was constantly overshadowed by the enormous task that lay ahead: being able to put a twist on everyday party food. Where would I start?

As with most new challenges I am faced with, I threw myself into it and made note after note, sketch after sketch – my mind was racing with the endless possibilities, the complex platters of edible delights, but the more I thought about it, the more my ideas and methods became obscured. In fact, by the time I had written my umpteenth word association with Pirates and Fairy Gardens, I knew I was heading down the wrong path.

It was time to stop, step back, take a break and get advice from the experts. 'Simple' was the word that kept coming up time and time again, 'keep it simple'. This book is something that should help parents through the party process – to give them some fun but simple ideas to brighten up a table of food. And so with an empty sketch pad and a sharpened pencil, I set about planning again.

The hardest part was to create something original, never been seen before, a punch-the-air-in-delight light bulb moment... an almost impossible task at times with the enormous amount of pictures found online by talented parents out there, who like me, just want to have fun with food. Every time I had an idea, I searched the internet looking for something similar, ready to punch the air having not found it or to have the wind knocked out of my sails by a like-minded parent.

There were, however, a couple of occasions when the light from my bulb initially flickered out, but these were ideas that were too good not to be included: great ideas that needed to be seen by a bigger audience. So I might not have been the first man on the moon, but the footprints I left there were all my own.

My first book, *Funky Lunch*, gained praise for including healthy ingredients and encouraging children to try new foods and while that still remains the ethos behind the Funky Lunch brand and what we deliver, we could not make a book about party food without including some sweet treats. I mean, what sort of children's party doesn't have chocolate, jelly and other sugary delights? We've tried to include ideas to cater for parties of all shapes and sizes, whether it is a small gathering at home, a large group of classmates in the village hall or a couple of friends round for afternoon tea. In fact, I wouldn't be surprised to see some of these ideas at a grown-up party, mixed in with the canapés and cheeseboard!

I feel very honoured having the opportunity to write these books and to work with the amazing people that have helped me. Yet at the same time I feel humbled that parents will want to buy it, be inspired and create food for their children that will become part of a special day.

I have no airs and graces, I'm not a cook by trade, I just love experimenting with food. I was discussing the journey that Funky Lunch has taken me on with a complete stranger recently and we were talking about writing the books and he said to me... 'This sounds fantastic, so are you a chef then?' 'No,' I replied, 'I'm just a dad'.

ladybird toasts

Exceedingly cute tomato-and-olive toasts.

makes 12 toasts

4 slices of wholemeal bread,
    toasted
low-fat cream cheese
Little Gem lettuce
6 baby plum tomatoes
small jar of black olives

Spread a thin layer of cream cheese on one side of each toasted slice of bread and then press down the lettuce leaves on top so they stick to and cover the bread.

Use a small circular or flower-shaped cookie cutter to cut out three shapes from each slice of bread and set aside.

To make each ladybird, take a baby plum tomato and cut it lengthways in half. Get a black olive and cut this in half to form the head. Trim the tomato and olives so they fit together snug on the lettuce leaf circle.

For the ladybird spots, cut some small circles of olive skin with a clean pen top or small cutter (press hard for a clean cut). Use two small dots of cream cheese for the eyes.

funk it up...

• If you are making a large number of these, you can speed things up, whizzing a load of olives to a smooth paste in a food processor. Then use a piping bag to squeeze dots of olive mixture on to the ladybirds back.
• You can also pipe the cream cheese for the eyes.
• Why not see what other insects you can make from a few similar ingredients?

'x' marks the spot

Fun pancakes for your little treasures.

makes approximately 16 pancakes

170g plain flour
pinch of salt
3 eggs
400ml milk
40g butter, melted
vegetable oil
to decorate
strawberries
dark chocolate, melted
   (or chocolate spread)

Mix the flour and salt together in a large bowl and then make a well in the centre and crack in the eggs.

Beat the eggs into the flour with a whisk and gradually beat in the milk to get a smooth liquid the same consistency as single cream.

Leave to stand for 15 minutes and when you are ready to cook, whisk through the melted butter.

Heat a little vegetable oil in a non-stick frying pan until hot, and pour in a ladleful of the batter mixture turning the pan quickly to evenly coat the base. Cook for between 30 seconds and a minute until the base is lightly browned.

Use a palette knife to gently flip the pancake over and cook on the other side for a few seconds until lightly browned. Slide the pancake onto a warm plate and repeat the process with the remaining batter.

To create your treasure map, cut a couple of thin slices of strawberry to make your 'X' and then take some melted dark chocolate in a piping bag and pipe some random dotted line paths all over the map leading to the treasure.

Finish off by piping a skull and crossbones and then placing some strawberry stalks as palm trees around the map.

birthday 'cakes'

Sweet looking sandwiches.

makes 12 sandwiches

white and brown bread
variety of sandwich fillings
to decorate
low-fat cream cheese
carrot
sweetcorn
red pepper
extras
paper cupcake cases
cup cake stand

Make up six standard sandwiches using the bread and fillings and then using a small round cookie cutter or egg cup, cut out four circles from each sandwich.

Stick two mini sandwiches on top of each other with cream cheese and place into a cup cake case and chill to keep fresh.

To prepare your cake toppings, cut twelve sticks of carrot about 4cm long and 5mm wide and then take some cheese slices, cut the same number of candle flames.

Using the red pepper, sweetcorn and any leftover carrot, either finely dice or use some small shaped cutters to create little vegetable shapes like hearts, diamonds, circles and flowers.

To assemble your cup cake sandwiches, spread an even layer of cream cheese across the top of each sandwich.

Decorate the top of each sandwich by cutting a small section from the top of each carrot candle and slotting a cheese flame into each. Make a hole in the top of each sandwich to stand the candle in position.

You can now decorate the rest of each sandwich using the small segments and shapes of pepper, sweetcorn and carrot.

Arrange the cupcake sandwiches on a stand or plate and use as the centrepiece for your party table.

monster burgers

A devilishly good snack.

feeds 6

1 small red onion, finely chopped
2 slices of wholemeal bread
   (crusts removed)
250g/9oz beef mince
$\frac{1}{2}$ tsp of thyme leaves
sunflower oil
6 mini hamburger buns
   (or small soft rolls)
to decorate
red pepper
cucumber or olives
cheddar cheese slices

Sauté the onion in 1 tablespoon of oil for 5 minutes until it is soft. Tear the bread into small pieces and put it into a food processor with the onion mixture and whizz together.

Combine the mince, thyme and onion mixture in a bowl and then divide into 6 equal portions. Roll each portion in a ball and then flatten into a burger shape.

Fry the burgers gently over a medium heat for about 4–5 minutes each side until cooked through. Alternatively, cook them under a preheated grill.

While your burgers are cooking, prepare the decoration by cutting two triangles of red pepper for horns and two circles of cucumber or olive for the eyes. Push the horns and eyes into the top half of the burger bun.

To make the teeth, cut a slice of cheese into a large circle and then around one edge cut a zigzag pattern

When your burgers are ready, place them on to the bun base and lay the cheese slice on top just off centre so the teeth hang over the edge of the burger. The heat of the burger will slowly melt the teeth and bend them downwards.

Finish it off with a blood thirsty drizzle of ketchup oozing from the mouth.

funk it up...

Why not create a different looking monster burger for each party guest by using different styles of horns and eyes.

almost eggstinct

They'll have a cracking adventure with these little dinosaur eggs.

makes 6–12 eggs

6 small eggs or 12 quail's eggs
  (to make them bite-sized)
half a shredded red cabbage
3 slice wholemeal bread
lettuce leaf, for decoration

Place the eggs in a saucepan with the shredded cabbage. You may need to do this in two batches to fit them all in.

Fill the pan with water until it just covers the eggs and then bring to a simmer and boil for 7 minutes. Once boiled, remove the eggs from the pan and cool under cold water.

Gently tap the eggs to create small cracks all over the shell and then return to the coloured water and leave for 2 hours.

To make the nest, gently cut your slices of bread into thin sticks of varying lengths and arrange on a baking tray.

Pre-heat the grill and then place the baking tray under the grill and toast the bread pieces. Keep a close eye on them to prevent burning and shake them halfway through to ensure they are toasted on all sides. Remove when golden brown.

Arrange your toasted bread in a bowl or on a plate in a random nest shape.

When your eggs have soaked for at least 2 hours, remove from the water and either place in the nest unpeeled or remove the shell to reveal your colourful patterned dinosaur eggs.

funk it up...

You can add a little bit of food colouring to the pan to vary the colours and make them more vivid.

nocturn·owls

These scotch eggs are a hoot.

makes 8 owls

4 small eggs
275g/10oz sausage meat
1 spring onion, finely chopped
1 tsp chopped fresh parsley
1 tsp thyme leaves
125g/4oz plain flour, seasoned
1 egg, beaten
125g/4oz breadcrumbs
oil for frying

to decorate
cucumber or black olives
cheese
orange pepper or carrot

Place the eggs in a saucepan of cold water, bring to the boil and then simmer for 9 minutes. Drain and cool under cold water, then peel.

Mix the sausage meat with the herbs and spring onion in a bowl and then season. Divide the mixture into four balls and flatten into a large oval shape about 5mm thick. Put the seasoned flour on a plate and roll each egg in it to cover and then place into the sausage meat and wrap around. Make sure the meat covers the egg completely and has a smooth surface.

Dip each sausage-covered egg into the beaten egg mixture coating it completely and then roll in the breadcrumbs to cover all over.

Heat some oil in a deep pan until a breadcrumb sizzles and turns brown when dropped in. Carefully place the Scotch egg into the hot oil and fry for 8–10 minutes until crisp and golden and the sausage meat is completely cooked.

Carefully remove and drain on kitchen paper and allow to cool.

Using a sharp knife cut the Scotch egg completely in half lengthways and set aside.

To decorate your owls, cut two small circles of cucumber skin or olive for the eyes and fill with a circle of cheese and an even smaller dot of cucumber skin for the pupils. Use a slice of carrot or orange pepper, and cut a triangle shape for the beak. Arrange your owls on a plate using some toasted bread or chopsticks for tree branches and a crescent moon shape slice of cheese.

funky smoothie

Lip-smackingly good refreshment.

makes 1 smoothie

handful of strawberries
banana
splash of 100% apple juice
squeeze of lime juice

to decorate
red grapes
bendy black straws
1 strawberry

Place the strawberries, banana, apple juice and lime juice into a blender and blend until smooth. If it is too thick, add a little more apple juice. Pour into a tall thin glass.

To create the lips, take your strawberry, remove the stalk and cut a small 'V' shape into the top. Round off the bottom section of the strawberry to finish the shape of the lips and then cut another 'V' shape across the front of the strawberry for the open mouth. Cut a small curved slit in the bottom of your strawberry and slide it over the lip of the glass.

Extend and bend two black straws and then with the drinking end, trim the straw to 1cm from the bend. Take a grape and cut about 1cm from the non-stalk end. Push the shortened drinking end of the straw through the grape and out the other side. You may need to blow down the straw to remove the piece of grape stuck in there. Repeat with the other straw so you have a pair of eyes.

Trim the other end of the straws so that when placed in the glass, the grape eyes just sit on top of the strawberry lips.

crudités towers

Tea-time toppling!

500g of carrots
dips of your choice, to serve

Cut the carrot into sticks of equal size and shape, approximately 8cm long and 1cm square. Be sure to keep the offcuts for nibbles!

how to play

Stack the blocks of carrot in rows of three, with the first level pointing north–south and the next level on top pointing east–west. Continue this pattern until all carrots have been used.

Decide who is going first and then that person must use only one hand to try to remove a stick of carrot from anywhere within the tower and then place it on the top of the tower following the same pattern.

The game continues by taking it in turns to remove sticks of carrot and placing them on the top to build a higher tower.

The winner is the last person to place a carrot stick on the top before it falls over.

Once the tower has toppled, it's time to tuck in!

wriggly dinner

They'll really dig this down-to-earth sausage 'n' mash treat.

feeds 4

1kg of potatoes, good for
   mashing
knob of butter and a splash of
   milk
handful of Cheddar cheese
8 thin chipolata sausages
a few florets of broccoli
a squeeze of honey

Pre-heat your grill to a medium heat.

Take the potatoes, butter and milk and make the mashed potato in your favoured way. Grate the Cheddar cheese into the mash according to taste and mix it in well.

Grill the sausages for 10–12 minutes, turning frequently until golden brown and cooked in the middle, then remove from the heat.

Steam the broccoli florets for 3–4 minutes, until just cooked and remove from the steamer.

To assemble your plate, spoon some cheesy mash into individual bowls or small side plates. Take the florets, one at a time, and push each into the mash, covering it completely.

Take two sausages and push them inbetween the florets and into the mash, just enough to hold them in position.

Give your 'worms' some eyes by sticking a thin slice of broccoli stem in place with some honey and then top with a dot of mash and a final broccoli tip.

camp fire crackles

Parsnip and potato crisps to munch on.

parsnips
sweet potatoes
olive oil

Preheat the oven to 200C.

Using a Y-shaped vegetable peeler, remove the outer skin of both the parsnips and sweet potatoes and discard.

Continue peeling both vegetables in long thin strips.

Line a baking tray with baking parchment and lay the vegetable strips out ensuring they do not overlap. (You may need to do this in batches.)

Lightly brush the vegetable strips with olive oil and then bake in the oven for approximately 15–20 minutes, turning halfway through, until they are crisp and golden.

Remove from the oven and transfer to kitchen paper to dry away any excess oil.

Once cooled, your vegetable strips should be light and crispy. Loosely arrange the crisps into a camp fire stack and serve.

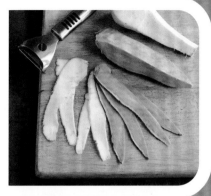

a dip in the ocean

Sail across the table with these guacamole boats.

makes 2 dips

1 ripe avocado, halved and
   stone removed
$1/2$ small red onion finely
   chopped
1 clove of garlic, grated
1 ripe tomato, chopped
juice of 1 lime
salt and black pepper, to taste
to serve
breadsticks
pitta bread

Carefully scoop out the avocado flesh into a bowl and mash well with a fork. Keep the shell.

Stir the onion, garlic, tomato and lime juice into the mashed avocado and season to taste.

Spoon the guacamole back into the empty avocado shells.

Slice open a pitta bread and then, from each slice, cut some sails by starting with a triangle shape and cutting a slight inward curve on two sides and curving the third side outwards.

Put the sails on a baking tray and pop under a preheated grill and toast for a few minutes, turning once until they are crisp.

Break a breadstick to about 8cm in length and stick it in the middle of your guacamole boat, then stand the pitta sails up in the mixture, leaning against the breadstick mast.

Use the pittas to dip into the guacamole when eating.

teepee treats

Set up camp round the party table and enjoy these crunchy filo pastries.

filo pastry sheets
melted butter, for brushing
milk chocolate

Preheat your oven to 180C.

Using some tin foil or baking parchment, make two or three cone shapes about 10cm high.

Take a sheet of filo pastry and cut it into 15cm squares.

Brush one sheet with melted butter and wrap around your cone shape tightly. Repeat this process with another 3 sheets, using melted butter to stick the sheets together and to hold all the edges down.

Stand your filo cones on a baking tray and bake in the oven for 4–5 minutes, until golden. Remove from the oven and allow them to cool.

Continue to make the filo cones until you have the amount you need.

Break the milk chocolate into a bowl over simmering water, stirring gently as it melts. Once done, very carefully place the melted chocolate into a piping bag.

Decorate them by piping an arched entrance at the bottom of one side and then a zigzag of chocolate near the top.

Pipe some long sticks of chocolate onto a baking sheet and chill until firm.

Trim the top of the cones and place some of the chocolate sticks inside, leaving them to poke proud of the top. Use any leftover chocolate shavings to build a campfire on the plate.

swamp jelly pots

Watch them sink their teeth into these funky jelly crocs.

1 packet of lime jelly
a few white marshmallows
a handful of grapes and raisins

Make the jelly according to the packet instructions and pour into small clear plastic cups or shot glasses and leave in the fridge to set.

Take the marshmallows and cut into strips. Then cut a serrated pattern along one edge to create the 'teeth'. Apply the marshmallows to the side of the cup (the cut edge of the marshmallow should stick to the side of the cup without too much effort).

To finish the crocodile, cut a grape into quarters. Make a slit into one of the cut edges of the grape and push half a raisin into the cavity. Repeat.

Sit the grape quarters onto the top of the jellies to create the eyes.

spuds-you-like

Fun baked jacket potato characters to liven any table.

makes 12 potatoes

12 small-/medium-sized baking
   potatoes
a little oil, for brushing
low-fat cream cheese
small jar of black olives
2 slices of ham

Preheat the oven to 200C.

Using a small circular cutter or a clean pen lid, carefully gouge out two 'eyes' near the top of each potato. Remove the eye piece leaving two holes about 5–10mm deep.

Brush the potatoes with a little oil and bake in a roasting tin for approximately 45–60 minutes, until crisp on the outside and fluffy in the middle. Remove the potatoes and allow them to cool to the touch.

Fill each 'eye socket' with a little cream cheese and then cut small circles from the olives for the pupils. Make a 'mouth' by taking a sharp knife and cutting a horizontal slit

below the eyes. Then take a small slice of ham, and poke inside the cavity, leaving a little sticking out to create a cheeky tongue.

funk it up...

To bring your potato people to life, use a selection of the following:

- red pepper slices
- cheese cubes
- cucumber slices
- broccoli florets
- herbs (parsley, chive or rosemary)
- cherry tomato
- sweetcorn

Take a few of your topping ingredients and use cream cheese to glue them into place. You can also make small holes in the surface of the potato and insert sticks, stalks and wedges of the above into place. Decorate them in the style of your choice and get the little ones involved too.

garden party

They won't be at snail's pace eating these.

cocktail sausages
375g ready-rolled puff pastry
a little Marmite
1 egg, beaten, to glaze
a few chives

Preheat the oven to 200C.

Roll out the puff pastry and cut strips about 4cm x 12cm and spread with Marmite.

At one end, place a cocktail sausage so that half of it is on the pastry and half is hanging over the end.

Fold the pastry over so that both edges touch and the sausage is held in place.

Spread a final thin layer of Marmite on top and then roll up from the non-sausage end until you reach the sausage and secure in place with a cocktail stick.

Brush with the beaten egg and place on a baking tray. Bake in the oven for 25 minutes until golden and crisp and the sausage is cooked through.

To decorate, trim some chives to 4cm and use a cocktail stick to poke two holes into the sausage 'head' and then insert the chives for the tentacles.

funk it up...

If Marmite is not your thing, then why not try a little tomato paste and finely grated cheese as your filling instead.

stars in their eyes

A healthy platter of stars and planets.

a selection of melons (such as watermelon, cantaloupe, Honeydew and Galia)

tools
melon baller
star- and moon-shaped cutters

Using a melon baller, scoop and cut various size melon balls to make your planets.

To create the Saturn ring, cut a slice of melon about 5mm thick and bigger than the melon ball. Cut out a large circle from the slice and then cut a smaller circle from the middle, the same size as the melon ball. Fit the ring of melon over the top.

Use the other shaped cutters or a sharp knife to create your solar system of stars and moons.

croak monsieur

These frog sandwiches will have them leaping for joy.

by Oscar Northeast, aged 7

makes 6 sandwiches

6 slices of brown bread
sandwich filling
ham slices
raisins
12 large green grapes
cucumber

Make up three rounds of sandwiches using the bread and preferred fillings. Cut two circles as large as you can from each sandwich.

Cut a grape in half and using a small knife, poke a hole in the front of each piece and then cut a small raisin in half and push each piece of raisin into the grape hole to make the pupils.

Take two slices of cucumber and cut each piece into a fan shape of three long toes.

Place the cucumber feet on your plate and then rest your round sandwich on top of the feet and put the eyes in place on top.

Finally, cut a long thin strip of ham and tuck one end into the sandwich and either roll the other end up to the mouth or extend the frog's tongue and place a raisin 'fly' on the tip.

flying saucers

Give them a close encounter with these simple snacks

makes 6 saucers

6 round crackers
cucumber
a few cherry tomatoes
cheese
a few black olives

To make one flying saucer, start with a single round cracker.

Cut a slice of cucumber and then using a small circular cutter, cut a circle of cucumber that fits on top of the cracker, but does not touch the edges

Cut a cherry tomato in half and place on top of the cucumber circle. Using a tiny cutter or sharp knife make some tiny discs of olive and stick these around the edge of the cherry tomato.

With a smaller circular cutter or clean pen lid, cut some little circles of cheese and set these around the edge of the cracker. Use some cucumber skin and add little dots on each small cheese circle for decoration.

To make the legs, take a wedge of cucumber and cut three pieces approximately 1cm square by 2.5cm in length.

Cut the base and top of each cucumber leg at an angle so that they tilt inwards when standing up. Sit the cracker on the top of the cucumber legs.

festive feast

A Yuletide spin on pizza.

large pizza base
1 jar of pizza topping sauce
Mozarella or feta cheese
red pepper
yellow pepper
a handful of spinach

Preheat the oven to 200C.

Take your pizza base and cut out a large Christmas-tree shape and then spread the base with some pizza topping sauce.

Using a small circular cutter, create some circles of red and yellow pepper.

Steam some spinach until just wilted and then decorate the tree with it and either some strips of Mozzarella or crumbled feta.

Finish the tree by adding the pepper, cut into the form of 'baubles' and a star for the top.

Bake in the oven for 10–15 minutes until the base is golden.

eye-scream

Have a chilling encounter with these fruity ice-cream treats.

handful of raspberries
icing sugar
handful of blueberries
**1 tub of good quality vanilla
    ice-cream**

Make a raspberry coulis by pushing
a few raspberries through a sieve
using the back of a spoon. Mix in a
little icing sugar to sweeten the
coulis and thicken it slightly.

Fill a small glass dish with a few
blueberries and raspberries and
then using a melon baller or small
ice-cream scoop, place a round ball
of ice cream on top of the dish.

Place a blueberry 'pupil' on top of
the ice-cream ball and then, using a
small spoon or syringe, drizzle the
raspberry coulis over the eyeballs to
create bloodshot veins.

yummy mummies

Pasta-embalmed meatball yumminess.

feeds 4

12 good quality meatballs
bag of dried tagliatelli
1 jar of tomato-based pasta
    sauce
black peppercorns
a little oil for frying

Using a shallow pan, lightly fry the meatballs for 10–12 minutes until golden brown and cooked through.

Meanwhile, fill a saucepan with cold water and bring to the boil. Add the tagliatelli and cook for 8–10 minutes according to packet instructions, until *al dente*.

When both the meatballs and pasta have cooked, allow them to cool slighty to the touch and then separate some strands of tagliatelli from the pan, take a meat ball and carefully wrap the pasta around the meatball like a bandage.

Repeat a couple more times until the meat ball cannot be seen. Poke a couple of peppercorns into the pasta for 'eyes'.

Heat some pasta sauce or passata in a pan and divide between 4 shallow bowls. Place 3 meatballs into each bowl of sauce and then warm through under a preheated medium grill.

This recipe was one of those moments where I'd thought I'd struck gold. The ink on my sketch of a pasta-wrapped meatball had hardly dried when I discovered a similar idea on the internet. It was an idea I had to share and so I must also urge you to visit the beautiful website I discovered, Gather and Nest, created and run by Cristine Roy. It is a great place to inspire parents.

flower power

These super-easy flower pot cakes will keep them in full bloom.

12 mini muffins in cases
1 chocolate Swiss roll cake
white chocolate buttons
milk chocolate buttons
raspberry jam
lollipop sticks

Take a muffin and carefully cut off the top of the muffin down to the paper case. Crumble up the cut-off muffin piece and then place back on top as 'soil'.

Use a sharp knife to cut slices from the Swiss roll about 1cm thick and lay flat on a surface.

Get some jam and stick the chocolate button 'petals' around the outside of the Swiss roll slice, adding an alternate colour button for the middle of the flower.

Using a lolly stick, carefully insert about 2cm of it into the slice of Swiss roll and then gently lift upright.

Insert the other end of the lolly stick in to the muffin pot and ensure it stands upright.

ca-tomato-pillar

They are going to *larva* this taste of Italy!

1 packet of cherry tomatoes
1 pot of Mozzarella balls
   (pearls)
a few black olives
handful of basil leaves
cocktail sticks (optional)

Build your caterpillars by taking
3 cherry tomatoes and two
Mozzarella balls and alternating
them on a plate. If you want to stop
them moving around, break a
cocktail stick into small pieces and
poke them into each piece to hold
them in place.

To decorate the caterpillar face, use
a thin slice of Mozzarella and cut
2 small circles and then add a small
dot of olive skin for the pupil.

To make the mouth, cut a small
circle of olive skin and then using
the same size cutter, cut a crescent
moon shape from the small circle.
Press this against the tomato face
and it should stick. If not, then use a
little low-fat cream cheese to hold
the face features in place.

Finally, tuck a basil leaf under the
head of each caterpillar.

*Caution: If you have used cocktail
sticks to hold the caterpillars
together, ensure that these are
safely removed before eating.*

bear claw bites

Steps of fun all the way!

makes 20

350g/12oz plain flour, plus
  extra for rolling out
1 tsp bicarbonate of soda
2 tsp ground ginger
1 tsp ground cinnamon
125g/4^1/$_2$oz butter
175g/6oz light soft brown
  sugar
1 free-range egg
4 tbsp golden syrup
raisins

Sift together the flour, bicarbonate of soda, ginger and cinnamon and pour into the bowl of a food processor. Add the butter and blend until the mix looks like breadcrumbs. Stir in the sugar.

Lightly beat the egg and golden syrup together, add to the food processor and pulse until the mixture clumps together. Tip the dough out, knead briefly until smooth, wrap in clingfilm and leave to chill in the fridge for 15 minutes.

Preheat the oven to 180C. Line two baking trays with greaseproof paper.

Take a piece of dough mixture about the size of a walnut and roll into a short fat sausage shape and then bend in the middle to make a slight 'V' shape.

Take more dough and make two egg shapes about the size of a marble, and then make two more of them slightly larger.

On the outside of the 'V', press a small lip around the edge and using a dab of water, press the egg shapes onto the edge and against the V. Place the two larger egg shapes in the middle and the smaller ones on either side.

Once they are all fixed in place, use a small sharp knife to cut an opening in the front of each one and then cut a raisin lengthways in half and push it into the opening leaving enough sticking out for a 'claw'.

Transfer the tray carefully to the oven and bake for 12–15 minutes, or until lightly golden-brown. Leave on the tray for 10 minutes and then move to a wire rack to finish cooling.

chicken pops

Cluckingly good savoury sensations.

makes 10

250g minced chicken or
   uncooked chicken breast
4 tbsp roughly cut breadcrumbs
1 tbsp ketchup
$\frac{1}{2}$ tsp dried oregano
1 egg, beaten
plain flour
fine breadcrumbs
to decorate
10 wooden sticks
red pepper
carrot
black olives
low-fat cream cheese or low-fat
   mayonnaise

Preheat the oven to 190C and line a baking sheet with parchment paper.

Mix the chicken mince, rough breadcrumbs, ketchup and oregano into a bowl by hand (if using chicken breast, pulse in a blender first).

Make the chicken balls. Fill a large bowl with cold water, put the beaten egg, flour and the fine breadcrumbs into separate shallow dishes. Dip your hands into the water first and then roll the chicken mixture into balls the size of walnuts (the water stops the chicken sticking to your hands). Next, roll the chicken into the flour, then the egg and finally the breadcrumbs. Continue rolling the chicken in a ball motion to remove the excess breadcrumbs and then place on the baking sheet. Bake for about 30 minutes until crisp and golden all over (cut into a spare one to check that they're cooked through). Leave to cool slightly.

While the chicken is cooking, prepare the decoration by cutting two small triangles of carrot for each 'mouth' and a three-pointed red pepper 'crown' for the top of the 'head'.

When the chicken is cool enough to handle, make a small hole on the top using a knife and push in the red pepper crown. Make another hole in the front of the chicken face and push the carrot in place to form an open beak.

Two dots of cream cheese or mayonnaise topped with small circles of olive will make the perfect 'eyes'.

funky games

Now they can play with their food!

bowl of wholegrain cereal
    squares
icing sugar
black and yellow food
    colouring

piping bag and small nozzle

Divide some icing sugar between the three bowls and add a little water to each to mix into a paste. Add a dash of black food colouring to one of the bowls to achieve a jet-black colour; add a pin-head amount of yellow colouring to another bowl to achieve a pale yellow colour. Leave the third bowl as just the icing sugar and water paste.

Divide the cereal squares in half.

To make the **dominoes**, take one half of the cereal squares and, using a small paint brush, paint one side of each square with the black icing. Put onto a plate and chill in the fridge until the icing is set. When the dominoes are at least touch-dry, put some of the white icing into a piping bag and, using a small nozzle, pipe the spots into place. Do random selections of numbers between zero (leave blank) and six at either end of each domino. The children can then match up the numbers like a game of dominoes.

To make the **letter tiles**, take the remaining cereal squares and, using a small paint brush. paint one side of each square with the pale yellow icing. Put onto a plate and chill in the fridge until the icing is set. When the tiles are at least touch-dry, put some of the black icing into a clean piping bag and write a selection of letters, one onto each tile. When these have dried the children can have fun creating words.

cracking treat

Fool them with these sweet boiled eggs!

makes 12 eggs

for the meringue
1 egg white
pinch of salt
50g castor sugar

for the filling
1 ripe mango, peeled, de-stoned
200g of low-fat Greek yoghurt
spoonful of honey
1 tsp of arrowroot or cornflour

for the soldiers
250g gingerbread dough
(see page 63 for recipe)

Preheat your oven to 150C and line a baking sheet with parchment paper.

Place the egg white and salt in a bowl and beat until fluffy. Gradually beat in the sugar until it is glossy and white and forms stiff peaks. Spoon out a tablespoon of mixture and push it off the spoon onto the baking sheet with your finger. The more dome-shaped and higher they are the more they will resemble egg shells. Shape your domes by dipping a finger into cold water and smoothing down any peaks. Alternatively, fill a piping bag and pipe out some domes straight onto the baking sheet.

Bake in the oven for 1 hour until cooked and crisp on the top. Remove and leave to cool completely.

To make the filling, sweeten the yoghurt by mixing in a spoonful of honey. Spoon the mixture into egg cups up to the rim and chill in the fridge.

Chop and purée the mango flesh with a blender. Place in a saucepan on the hob and add a teaspoon of arrowroot or corn flour. Heat gently, stirring occasionally until it thickens. Remove from the heat and allow to cool.

Remove the egg cups from the fridge and use a teaspoon to remove a little of the yoghurt mixture from the centre. Spoon the mango 'yolk' into this 'well'.

To make the soldiers, roll out your gingerbread dough to a thickness of 5mm and cut out lots of rectangles approximately 8cm x 2cm. Place onto a baking sheet and bake in a 180C-preheated oven for 12 minutes until golden. Remove from the oven and allow them to cool.

Top each egg cup with a meringue and serve with 2–3 soldiers for dunking.

arctic delights

A polar expedition worth the trek!

by Izzy Northeast, aged 9

makes 12 bears

4 packets of white chocolate
  buttons
packet of desiccated coconut
12 strawberries
a few squares of plain
  chocolate

Set aside 24 white chocolate buttons for the 'ears' and melt the rest of the chocolate buttons in a glass bowl either over simmering water or in a microwave.

Get a shallow dish and pour enough coconut in to cover the base.

When the melted chocolate has cooled a little, push a fork or small skewer into the stalk end of a strawberry and dip it into the chocolate, turning to coat it all over. Then quickly roll the chocolate-covered strawberry in the coconut, making sure that all the chocolate is covered and that the coconut sticks and holds in place. Tap the strawberry gently to remove any excess coconut and place on a plate.

Repeat with the rest of the strawberries (you may have to warm the chocolate up a few times if it starts to firm up). Once all of the strawberries are covered in the coconut, put the plate into the fridge until the chocolate has set.

To decorate the polar bear face, melt a few squares of plain chocolate and spoon the cooled melted chocolate into a piping bag. Squeeze out two dots for the eyes and then a round triangle shape for the nose.

To finish off, cut two slits into the strawberry behind the eyes on the top of the head. Insert a white chocolate button into each slit for the ears.

blooming marvellous

Pretty mini flower-shaped sandwiches.

bread slices
variety of sandwich fillings
to decorate
a selection of:
cucumber slices
red and yellow pepper
tomato slices
carrots slices
sweet corn
cress
equipment
flower-shaped cutter, circular
   cutters, apple corer and
   sharp knife

Make up enough sandwiches for your party and then, allowing one sandwich per child, cut one or two flower shapes from each sandwich. If you don't have a flower-shaped cookie cutter then start with a circle and working around the edge, trim five small 'V' shapes to leave you with the flower shape. You could round off the edges with a clean pair of scissors.

Using a smaller circular cutter or apple corer, remove a circle from the centre of the top layer of each sandwich, so you can see the filling through the hole.

Fill each hole with a variety of topping ingredients to decorate the inner flower circle, combining tomato and cress stems or using sweet corn on top of a tuna sandwich.

funk it up...

To create a 'meadow' of flowers, take a large foil platter and turn it upside-down to create a curved hill and then cover with leafy lettuce.

Cover the platter in your array of flower sandwiches and finish off with a few sprigs of cress, parsley or chives as blades of grass.

up, up and away

Sandwiches they won't want to let go of.

makes 8 balloons

4 slices of wholemeal bread
low-fat cream cheese
carrot
various colourful toppings like:
cucumber
cheddar slices
smoked salmon
red and yellow pepper

First cut the oval balloon shapes from your slices of bread (cut around a small glass using a sharp knife, extending one end into a more oval 'point'). You should be able to get two balloon shapes from each slice of bread. Repeat this process until you have 8 balloons. These are 'open' sandwiches, so you'll need just one slice of bread from which to cut the balloon shape.

Spread each balloon with some low-fat cream cheese and then top with a variety of different sandwich toppings to get a colourful selection.

Trim any over-hang of topping with a sharp knife or clean pair of scissors.

To make the balloon string, take a carrot and peel a long thin strip from it using a vegetable peeler. Trim the carrot strip with a knife until it is the width of a matchstick. Alternatively, use a zester and peel a couple of lengths of carrot.

Place all your balloon sandwiches on a platter and tuck the carrot string underneath.

funky tip...

Cut your carrot strings first and soak them in a bowl of cold water while you make the balloon sandwiches. The strips of carrot will be more flexible after soaking and easier to curve.

snow shake

A winter wonderland drink.

vanilla ice cream or
mint ice cream
glass of milk or natural
yoghurt
green food colouring
(optional)
desiccated coconut
honey

Start by decorating the glass and then leaving it to chill. To do this, squeeze a blob of honey on a plate and, with a thin paintbrush, paint a snowflake shape onto the outside of the glass. Then paint a thin line of honey around the lip of the glass.

On a separate plate spread a layer of desiccated coconut out and dip the lip of glass in the coconut ensuring it sticks all the way around. Pick up the rest of the coconut with your fingers and sprinkle it onto the snowflake shape you painted, gently tapping the glass to allow the loose pieces to fall off. Once your glass decoration is finished, pop it in the fridge to harden the honey and set the coconut.

Put the ice cream and milk into a blender and whizz until smooth. To get a slightly green colour, add a couple of drops of green food colouring and mix in. As an alternative, you could use mint ice-cream instead of vanilla, this will give a green colour without the need for extra colouring.

Slowly pour in the ice cream milkshake so it fills the glass and covers the snowflakes. These should now be visible against the green coloured drink.

funky thanks

It's that part of the book where I am happy to take a step back and allow others to shine.

First up is Mr Matt Inwood of Absolute Press, the man with a thousand job roles, but only one job title and the driving force behind this book. My mentor, my timekeeper and my 2am e-mail buddy – and I thought I worked hard! I can't thank you enough.

To the rest of the team at Absolute Press and Bloomsbury Publishing who have given me yet another amazing chapter in my life: thank you.

A recipe book is just pages of ideas and words until you put it in the hands of some very talented people. To Gen and Jason: your understanding of this project was second to none and to work with you both has been a huge pleasure and great learning experience. Thank you.

To my wife, Lisa, and the two brightest lights in my life, Izzy and Oscar: thank you for tasting some random-looking recipe attempts and letting me lock myself away at the weekends to work on the book. I think you finally understand the phrase, 'Do not disturb'!

To Mum and Dad: thank you for your guidance and support over the years. I hope I continue to make you proud no matter how crazy this journey becomes.

To my special Funky Lunch fan club: you are a select group of ladies who have been my playground mums, my sounding board, my loud hailers, my supporters and my friends. Thank you Mrs P, Stacey, TC, Lu, Suze, Katie, Sarah and Clare.

And, finally, to the rest of my family, my friends, the Facebook and Twitter followers: your support and continued feedback helps to keep me moving *Funky Lunch* forward, and for that reason alone, I thank you.